Crayola World of
YELLOW

Mari Schuh

Lerner Publications ◆ Minneapolis

For my bright, cheery friend Kaelyn

Official Licensed Product
Lerner Publications Company
A division of Lerner Publishing Group, Inc.
241 First Avenue North
Minneapolis, MN 55401 USA

For reading levels and more information, look up this title at www.lernerbooks.com.

Main body text set in Mikado a Medium 20/28.
Typeface provided by HVD Fonts.

Library of Congress Cataloging-in-Publication Data

Names: Schuh, Mari C., 1975– author. | Crayola (Firm)
Title: Crayola world of yellow / by Mari Schuh.
Other titles: World of yellow
Description: Minneapolis : Lerner Publications, [2020] | Series: Crayola world of color | Audience: Ages 5–9. | Audience: K to grade 3. | Includes bibliographical references and index.
Identifiers: LCCN 2018042626 (print) | LCCN 2018043858 (ebook) | ISBN 9781541561410 (eb pdf) | ISBN 9781541554689 (lb : alk. paper)
Subjects: LCSH: Yellow—Juvenile literature. | Color in nature—Juvenile literature. | Colors—Juvenile literature. | Crayons—Juvenile literature.
Classification: LCC QC495.5 (ebook) | LCC QC495.5 .S3687229 2020 (print) | DDC 535.6—dc23

LC record available at https://lccn.loc.gov/2018042626

Manufactured in the United States of America
1-45786-42668-12/5/2018

CONTENTS

Hello, Yellow!

Do you see **yellow** around you?

Our world is full of beautiful yellow. Gold, canary, and lemon are all shades of yellow.

Yellow **in Nature**

Yellow lights up the sky! The golden sun shines brightly on a warm summer day. Leaves glow in the trees.

Some leaves turn yellow in the fall.
Slowly, they fall to the ground.

See them pile up!

Sunflowers grow tall in a country field. Their flowers move toward the sun.

Yellow **Animals**

Yellow crawls across the ground. The bright skin of lizards and salamanders stands out against the grass.

See yellow buzzing around colorful flowers. Bumblebees sip sweet nectar.

Cheep! Cheep!

Yellow can be soft and fluffy. Cute chicks have fuzzy feathers called down.

Yellow **Foods**

People enjoy yellow foods at picnics. Squirt yellow mustard on a corn dog. Snack on sweet peppers!

Spread butter on corn on the cob.
Yellow is so yummy!

Yellow **Where You Live**

Yellow takes you where you need to go! Catch a taxi in the city, or ride to school in a yellow school bus.

Yellow signs help people on the road. They show us where to turn and where to cross. The bright color warns drivers to be careful.

Yellow is fun! Ride down a yellow slide. Wear a yellow uniform to play your favorite sport.

Where else can you see yellow?

Color with Yellow!

Draw a picture using only yellow crayons. What will you draw? How many shades will you use?

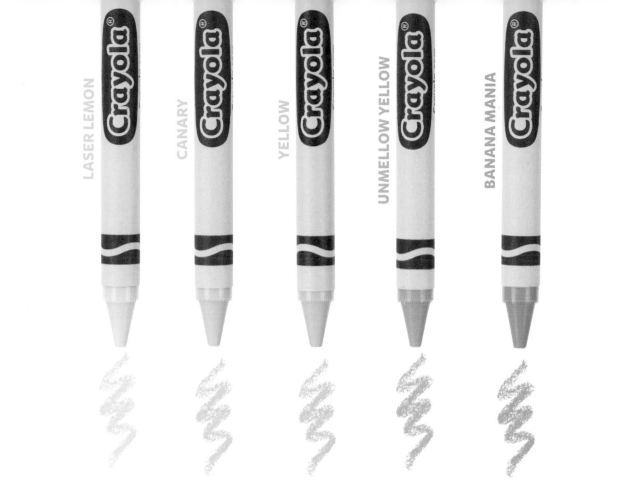

LASER LEMON

CANARY

YELLOW

UNMELLOW YELLOW

BANANA MANIA

Yellow All around You

Yellow is almost everywhere! Here are some Crayola® crayon shades of yellow used in this book. Can you find them in the photos?

Glossary

down: a bird's soft, fluffy feathers

nectar: a sweet liquid that is found in many flowers

shade: a color's lightness or darkness

taxi: a car with a driver whom people pay to take them where they want to go

uniform: special clothing worn by sports teams and other groups

To Learn More

Books

Leaf, Christina. *Yellow Animals*. Minneapolis: Bellwether Media, 2019.
Explore the color yellow by reading about yellow animals.

Schuh, Mari. *Crayola Fall Colors*. Minneapolis: Lerner Publications, 2018.
Discover all the colors you can find during fall, including the color yellow!

Websites

Crayola Coloring Page: Corn and Flowers
https://www.crayola.com/free-coloring-pages/print/corn-and-flowers-coloring-page/
Visit this website to color pretty flowers and corn in shades of yellow.

Yellow Coloring Page
http://www.kidzone.ws/prek_wrksht/colors/colors-yellow1.htm
Enjoy coloring different things that are yellow!

Index

Photo Acknowledgments

Image credits: Roman Samokhin/Shutterstock.com, p. 2; Nadezda Nikitina/Shutterstock.com, p. 4 (fish); SERGIY KUBYK/Shutterstock.com, p. 4 (duck); bergamont/Shutterstock.com, p. 4 (bananas); Tsekhmister/Shutterstock.com, p. 5 (chicks); mihalec/Shutterstock.com, p. 5 (combine); Ranglen/Shutterstock.com, p. 6; Chas Breton/Barcroft Media/Getty Images, pp. 6–7; Robert CHG/Shutterstock.com, pp. 8–9; Milos Batinic/Shutterstock.com, p. 9; salajean/Shutterstock.com, pp. 10–11; Christian Schoissingeyer/Shutterstock.com, p. 12; Rainer Kaufung/McPhoto/ullstein bild/Getty Images, pp. 12–13; HelloRF Zcool/Shutterstock.com, pp. 14–15; Kirill Zatrutin/Shutterstock.com, pp. 16–17; Kwangmoozaa/Shutterstock.com, p. 18; GreenArt/Shutterstock.com, pp. 18–19; GMVozd/E+/Getty Images, pp. 20–21; Kovaleva_Ka/Shutterstock.com, p. 21; Mike Focus/Shutterstock.com, p. 22; Tupungato/Shutterstock.com, pp. 22–23; Ken Hurst/Shutterstock.com, p. 24; BT.Suksan/Shutterstock.com, pp. 24–25; romrodinka/iStock/Getty Images, pp. 26–27; PNC/DigitalVision/Getty Images, p. 27; Studio Barcelona/Shutterstock.com, p. 28 (left); Yellow Stocking/Shutterstock.com, p. 28 (right); zorina_larisa/Shutterstock.com (design elements throughout).

Cover: gornjak/Shutterstock.com (sunflowers); AlinaMD/Shutterstock.com (sunrise); Kichigin/Shutterstock.com (bee); Richard Peterson/Shutterstock.com (chick).